GREEK ISLANDS
FOR
TRAVELERS

-The total guide-

The comprehensive traveling guide for all your traveling needs.

PUBLISHED BY

Table of Contents

Why do we claim our guides are "total guides"?

Chapter 1: Why visit the Greek Islands?

Chapter 2: Greek Islands local travel advice

Chapter 3: The Greek Islands on a budget

Chapter 4: Greek Islands travel basics

Chapter 5: Transportation opportunities on the Greek Islands

Chapter 6: The best hotels and restaurants on the Greek Islands

Chapter 8: Shopping on the Greek Islands

Chapter 9: The portrait of the Greek Islands

PS: Please leave your review

Why do we claim our guides are "total guides"?

Why are they really comprehensive?

Because we do almost anything to make sure that all the main issues relevant to the conscious traveler are covered in our guides.

We hate the typical boring travel guides chocked up with standard information you can readily find on the Internet.

We travel, we research other guides, we talk to locals, we ask friends, we ask friends of friends,

we do whatever it takes to make sure that we have you covered. All the angles! This is how we get the best tips, the most valuable for every one of our travel destinations.

That is where we got the best tips, the most valuable ones about our travel destinations.

All our guides are reviewed and edited by a "local" writer to make sure that the guide is one of its kind, comprehensive, fun and interesting. We prefer not to add too many maps or photos since you can have all that on the internet. We prefer to focus the content on tips and unique data that makes worthwhile to buy our total guides.

We use different approaches for each city, as each destination is unique. You will be able to verify that our guides are not standardized. Each one is different because each place is different. And you will enjoy the difference,

Our production team is very proud of our guides. We hope you will enjoy the reading and take full advantage of your traveling.   !

Chapter 1: Why visit the Greek Islands?

Credits: Pixabay.com

Whenever someone is considering a visit to the Greek Islands, an idyllic image comes to mind – walking on the pebbled shores, taking in the salty air and feeling hopelessly romantic as you look at the islands beautifully displayed on the horizon. The truth is that the Greek Islands are popular among tourists of different ages and backgrounds, with hundreds of reasons backing up this destination. Whether you are interested in spending your holiday at the beach bar or you want to discover more of the Greek universe, it is guaranteed that you will have an amazing time during your stay on any of the Greek Islands.

For many people, a visit to the Greek Islands goes further than the beach. They know that Greece, together with its islands, has so much more to offer. You can get lost walking through traditional villages, reconnect with God by visiting the countless monasteries in the area and check out some of the finest museums in the world. Apart from that, you will definitely fall in love with the laid-back lifestyle that is characteristic on the islands. Add to that affordable hotels and a world-class dining experience at traditional Greek taverns and you have a complete experience.

If you want to discover the Greek Islands from a completely different perspective, you can always consider a cruise. In this way, you will be able to cover some of the most important islands that Greece has to offer, such as Corfu, Santorini, Mykonos, Crete, Rhodes, Skiathos and Hydra. There are numerous companies that you can contact for a cruise in the Greek Islands, so do not hesitate to take that opportunity into account.

On the other hand, if you decide to visit only one island, you will have the opportunity to discover it in detail. You can take as much time as you want, walking through the narrow streets and checking out the beautiful whitewashed houses. You can walk on the sandy beaches and spend relaxing days under a beach umbrella. There is no greater feeling in the world than taking a dip in the warm, yet salty waters of the Aegean Sea. In the afternoon, you can visit the bustling harbors and check out the local folks, while enjoying an iced coffee. For dinner, a rustic tavern is the ideal place and you will certainly enjoy the great conversation with the owners (the Greeks are genuinely friendly people). As the sun gradually dives into the sea, you will know that you have chosen the right destination for your visit. Apart from that, you can always rent an ATV and discover the secluded parts of the islands. Many of these islands also have ancient sights that are great to discover, so you can really have an amazing time.

Greece is reputed for its islands – even though there are over 6000 islands and islands, only 227 are inhabited and even few are chosen by tourists. The majority of the Greek Islands are located on the Aegean

Sea, while only a few correspond to the Ionian Sea. The Ionian Islands are often selected as a holiday destination and I especially recommend the island of Corfu; here, on this island, you really have it all – amazing, ancient architecture; landscapes that are more beautiful than you could ever imagine and beaches that are perfect for relaxation.

If you are looking to take delight into the island charm but you do not want something overcrowded with tourists, you should consider the Saronic Gulf Islands. Hydra is the obvious choice when it comes to these islands – the tourists who visit this island fall in love with the relaxing atmosphere (no cars to disturb your peace and quiet). Hydra also has some pretty amazing beaches, not to mention the charming harbor which is perfect for afternoon strolls. A less touristy, but nevertheless interesting choice is represented by the Sporades Islands. I invite you to visit Evia Island, discovering luscious vegetation and a peaceful atmosphere.

The Cyclades are some of the most popular Greek Islands and you definitely have every reason to visit them, especially if you want to discover the typical Greek atmosphere. Two of the most popular islands are Mykonos and Santorini. The first one is actually a fishing village but it has amazing beaches and plenty of opportunities for relaxation. Apart from that, at a close distance from Mykonos, you can visit Delos, which is one of the most important archeological sites in Greece. Santorini is an island that delights you in every step of the way, whether we are talking about the geological aspect or the idyllic villages located on the rim of the volcano crater.

No matter which of the Cyclades you decide to visit, you will see that they all have specific elements to entice you with. Starting with the whitewashed houses with blue windows and doors and continuing with the rocky landscapes, these Greek Islands are seductive to say the least. Tourists return to them for their delightful beaches, not to mention the traditional elements of culture, such as the perfectly-preserved windmills.

The Dodecanese Islands are also worth visiting as they are the perfect blend between two cultures, due to their proximity to Turkey. If you are looking for a unique experience, the island of Rhodes is the ideal destination. A more remote choice is represented by the North Aegean Islands – I recommend visiting the island of Samos, as it is close to Turkey as well and you can check out the ancient site of Ephesus.

A visit to the Greek Islands would not be complete without Crete. This is the biggest island and certainly one that has many things to offer to its visitors. Leaving aside the amazing beaches and the crystal-clear sea, you will definitely have a full calendar – there are ancient Minoan ruins to be discovered, picturesque mountain scenery to be taken in and rustic villages to be visited. Tourists are also enticed by the wealth of dramatic caves that the island of Crete has to offer, not to mention the beautiful gorges (be sure to check out the renowned Samaria Gorge).

Chapter 2: Greek Islands local travel advice

Credits: Pixabay.com

If you have decided to visit the Greek Islands, one of the first things you need to remember is that you will need to travel by ferry or boat. The majority of the ferries leave from the mainland, from Athens. You can also use the ferry or the boat in order to travel from one island to the other. In regard to the price of the ticket, the closer the islands, the cheaper the ticket is going to be. The good news is that the tickets can be booked and paid in advance. In this way, you can eliminate a lot of the stress associated with the journey and beat the rest of the crowd looking to get the last minute tickets. The Saronic Gulf Islands are closest to Athens, which means that this is the cheapest journey you can undertake.

When choosing the Greek Islands for a summer holiday, most people think about sunbathing and relaxation. However, there are plenty of island activities that one can become engaged in, including kayaking and parasailing. An active holiday can also include trips with the banana boats, exploring remote areas of the islands with ATVs and diving trips.

On the island of Karpathos, you can take part in dives that are organized in sea caves – you can visit http://www.divingkarpathos.gr/ and obtain more information on the subject. Or, if you want, you can check out http://www.milosdiving.gr/ and see for yourself what diving on the island of Milos is all about. The diving experience is going to provide you with an amazing opportunity to see dolphins, monk seals and deep-sea fish species. As for snorkeling, the best islands for such activities include Paros and Kastellorizo. The latter is more remote but it is definitely worth a visit, especially if you are passionate about snorkeling.

Speaking about outdoor activities, hiking the Samaria Gorge can prove out to be one of those life-changing experiences you have always wanted to try out. Any outdoor enthusiast will want to go on this hiking experience, not only for testing one's physical limits but also because this is one of the most beautiful landscapes that Greece has to offer. You can take some pretty amazing photographs and the workout is definitely worth it. On the plus side, everyone is coming to the Greek Islands to bathe in the sun, so it is guaranteed there will not be many tourists following the hiking trail.

If you are looking for an experience like no others, I recommend visiting the island of Zakynthos. Here, you can become a volunteer for the Sea Turtle Protection Society and work with qualified personnel in order to protect endangered sea turtles. This experience will remain in your mind forever and you feel great knowing that you have brought your own contribution to such a critical manner. Speaking about eco-tourism opportunities, do not hesitate to visit the island of Mesta and see how beautiful this part of Greece actually is.

The beach is the number one reason that brings tourists to the Greek Islands. Both sandy and pebbled beaches are visited by an impressive number of tourists each year, all of them looking for the same thing – to bask in the sun. Greek Islands such as Crete, Santorini and Corfu entice prospective tourists with amazing beaches and the opportunity to soak in the sun, while admiring the crystal-clear sea. Santorini is the perfect island for couples, honeymooners included. Apart from the unique volcanic scenery, the island of Santorini entices with the prospective opportunities for camping on the beach. During your stay in Santorini, it is highly recommended to go on a winery tour and try out scuba diving. Other Greek Islands with great beaches include Mykonos, Naxos, Thasos, Rhodes and Skiathos. Rhodes and Corfu also have amazing medieval fortresses that are totally worth a visit.

If you are interested in a great night life and parties, I recommend going to the island of Ios. Both Mykonos and Santorini are also well known for the night life but nothing beats the island of Ios and the amazing parties that are organized there. If you want to meet young people looking to have a great time, this is the right destination for you to visit. The parties continue till dawn and there are amazing, traditional Greek beverages and cocktails to be enjoyed. On the other hand, if you are interested in getting off the beaten track, you should consider visiting the islands of Rhodes and Kos. Corfu remains one of the most popular destinations for backpackers – so, if you want to go through a journey that is a rite of passage, this island is more than perfect for such experiences.

Regardless of the Greek Islands that you decide to visit, there is one thing that you must remember. There are many other tourists who are interested in the same destinations, looking to book their own accommodation. The Greek Islands are extremely crowded during the summer period and you might have the surprise of not finding anything available. If you want to protect yourself against such problems, it is for the best that you book your accommodations as early as it is possible. In fact, make sure that you book all the services you want to benefit from in advance as well (ferry transportation and outdoor activities included).

August is the month when the majority of the tourists come to the Greek Islands. It is also the month in which there is a beautiful full moon to be enjoyed. For this reason, you will have the pleasant surprise to discover that many of the tourist attractions – including the archaeological sites and the museums – stay open late. As a visitor to any of the Greek Islands, you will have the opportunity to visit some of the most important historic sites in the light of the full August moon. This year's event is going to take place on the 29th of August, so be sure to mark it on your calendar.

Chapter 3: The Greek Islands on a budget

Credits: Pixabay.com

Despite what you have heard about the Greek Islands, it is possible to travel to this destination without having to pay a fortune. In planning your vacation to any of the Greek Islands, one of the most important things you need to take into consideration is the accommodation. While many of the Greek Islands present luxurious, five-star hotels, there are plenty of cheap accommodation options available as well. Let's find out more information on the subject.

If you are traveling with a group, it is recommended that you consider hostels for your accommodation. Otherwise, you can choose to rent a studio apartment, enjoying the amazing views and the bargain prices at which these are offered. Apart from that, it is possible to negotiate the price of the accommodation, especially if you are interested in a prolonged stay. These studios have their own kitchen or kitchenette, which also means that you can save a lot of money by cooking yourself. Instead of going out to dinner every night, you can purchase what you need at the grocery store and prepare a delicious meal on your own. The leftovers can be used the next day for lunch, so you will be able to save even more money. As you will have the opportunity to see for yourself, the food at the supermarket is clearly cheaper than the already-prepared dishes at the restaurant. The same goes for the alcohol, so you may want to pay attention to that as well. The street food – sandwiches and gyros – is not only cheap but also delicious. Moreover, there are plenty of fresh fruits and vegetables that can be purchased from the street.

For those of you who are planning on renting out a bigger apartment, keep in mind that the costs of the accommodation can be split with another couple or group of friends. In regards to the travels on the island, you can save a lot of money by renting out ATVs or scooters; small cars can be rented at affordable prices as well. Be sure to check at your hotel, as there are some hotels that can provide special deals on the above-mentioned rental services. The public buses are also an alternative for the budget-conscious but you need to remember is that they are very slow and it can take some considerable time until you will reach the desired destination.

Camping provides one of the best opportunities when it comes to saving money on the accommodation. On some of the islands, you have the pay a cheap price for pitching your tent but, on most of the islands, beach camping is free and it can be quite an amazing experience. If you decide to pitch your tent on a specialized campground, there are certain facilities you will benefit from, including Wi-Fi. In the Cyclades, there is the Kyklades Camping, which is actually a network of seven campgrounds. These are located in Paros, Naxos, Ios, Mykonos, Syros, Milos and Thira. On each of these campgrounds, you can find a brochure –

this brochure actually provides discounts for each of the campgrounds you decide to spend your time at.

The trip to the Greek Islands can be quite pricey, especially if you choose expensive flights or wait until the last minute to arrange for the travel. Luckily, there are more and more cheap carriers landing on smaller airports. Instead of flying from your country to Athens and spending a fortune on the ticket, you can find cheaper tickets for Thessaloniki. It is also useful to book the ferry tickets in advance; as you will see on your own, the prices are more expensive when purchased on the spot than booked on advance. It is also worth mentioning that the slower ferries are cheaper in price – so, if you are under a tight budget and not in a hurry, you can consider the transportation that takes a little bit longer. You can also consider booking the accommodation through a specialized agency – in this way, it will become their job to get you on the island and they will handle the ferry transfer, leaving you to enjoy the arrival.

When making the arrangements for your accommodation, you might also inquire about the transportation from the ferry to the hotel. If you have decided to stay at a hotel, you need to at least make sure that the transfer is offered for free. For those who are interested in taking different tours of the chosen island, Viator (http://www.viator.com/) is a great resource to visit. Apart from the island tours, this company provides round-trip ferry transportation from Athens at awesome prices (especially if you decide to travel with the slower ferry – 8 hours one-way travel). On the island of Corfu, and not only, you can save an important sum of money by choosing the bike rental services. Plus, the bike is a great way of exploring the island.

When shopping on the Greek Islands, you can go the extra mile and spend a few moments talking to the local shop owners. Apart from getting to know new people and immerse into their culture, you might have the pleasant surprise of being offered a discount for your shopping.

While this might sound obvious, if you want to save money on your travels, you need to avoid visiting the Greek Islands during the peak season. The months of July and August are the most crowded – even though the prices are practically tripled during that period, you will have the surprise to see that everything is booked solid. If you want to save a lot of money, come in September or even at the start of October. The prices are genuinely amazing, the weather is still great and you can enjoy a peaceful vacation, as there are not so many tourists choosing that time of year for a visit to the Greek Islands. The combination of empty beach, hot weather and cheap prices is definitely worth to be taken into consideration.

Each of the Greek Islands has something different to offer to the budget-conscious traveler. The island of Ios welcomes budget travelers and especially backpackers, enticing them with cheap food and drinks, not to mention amazing accommodation opportunities. At Naoussa, on the island of Paros, one can enjoy the most delicious and yet inexpensive seafood. Plus, the island is completely peaceful and it does not cost anything to watch the fishing boats go about their business.

For those with a passion for the outdoors, there are numerous hiking trails that are free to be explored and enjoyed. For the famous Samaria Gorge, you will have to pay approximately six Euros but it is totally worth it to be included in the budget. It is also possible to save money by choosing to stay on a lesser known island – as it was already mentioned, Greece has many beautiful islands and the ones that are less known as just as beautiful. On the plus side, there are not as many tourists and you can enjoy the peaceful atmosphere to the maximum.

Chapter 4: Greek Islands travel basics

Credits: Pixabay.com

When planning your trip to the Greek Islands, there are a few things you need to take into consideration. Throughout this chapter, you will find the travel basics that are necessary for such a trip. Be sure to read until the very last paragraph and organize your to-do list,

25

according to the information included within this chapter.

Greece is part of the European Union, so the currency is Euro. Given the most recent changes that Greece has gone through, it is recommended that you carry cash as well. You can exchange money at the bank or at the different exchange offices but be sure to check for the commission (reading the fine print is always a good idea). As a citizen coming from the European Union, all you need to enter Greece is a valid ID card. If you are coming from countries outside the EU, you will require a valid passport. There are no visas required for the Greek Islands and you are allowed to stay for a maximum period of 3 months; if you are interested in a longer stay, you will have to apply for a residence permit.

It is very important to understand that each country has its customs. When it comes to indecent behavior, the Greeks are very strict. Regardless of which Greek Island you decide to visit, you should refrain from rowdy or indecent behavior. The same goes for excessive drinking – depending on the situation, you might have to pay a heavy fine or even go to prison for a short period of time. Always remember that indecent behavior is not tolerated.

When traveling to the Greek Islands, it is highly recommended that you get both the travel and the medical insurance. The travel insurance can protect you against theft, lost luggage and other things like that. The medical insurance can cover any medical emergencies you might require during your stay. For medical emergencies, you can also consider the European Health Insurance Card. This is free and you can obtain it from your own country, before the actual card. Keep in mind, however, that this card is valid only for emergencies (you will also have to sign a document stating that you did not travel to the respective country for that specific treatment and it was indeed an emergency). The treatment opportunities are somewhat limited on certain Greek Islands, especially when it comes to the number of ambulances available. Emergency medical assistance can be requested by dialing 112 or 166 on your phone.

In regard to the crime rate, the Greek Islands are relatively safe. However, you should pay increased attention in the crowded tourist places, as there is a risk for petty theft. It is also a good idea to avoid the areas that are more remote or secluded, the parks in particular. As a woman, you should not accept rides from people you do not know – there have been many reports of sexual assaults that have occurred in this way. You should also avoid displaying expensive equipment in public and the same goes for cash. When stopping at a traffic light, be sure to lock your doors and keep your bags out of sight. There are many petty thieves just waiting for the opportunity to snatch your bags. It is recommended that you do not carry the credits cards, travel documents and cash in the same bags; if your hotel has a safe, you can store your valuables and some spare cash there. The women should keep their purse in front of them and not on the shoulder, especially when traveling to the more crowded areas.

If you have decided to rent a car during your stay on the Greek Islands, check its condition and make sure that it is fit to drive. Also, if you are required to leave your passport as security, be sure to refuse. For driving mopeds, you will need a valid A1 license. When renting scooters, mopeds or motorcycles, you will also require wearing a crash helmet. If you do not wear the required helmet, you can get a heavy fine. Moreover, if you are involved in an accident, not wearing the helmet might actually invalidate the travel insurance. While drinking excessively is frowned upon, if you drive and drink over the existing limit, you can receive a heavy fine or even a prison sentence.

Driving on any of the Greek Islands can prove out to be quite a dangerous experience, as the majority of the drivers are reckless and quite aggressive. You need to pay increased attention to the road, as there is a lot of difficult terrain, with narrow curbs and heavy traffic. As a pedestrian, you need to be extra careful when crossing the road, as not many drivers stop when seeing a crossing sign. All drivers require a valid license to drive on the Greek Islands. All passengers in the car are obliged to wear the seatbelt at all times.

Many of the beaches on the Greek Islands have specific policies regarding swimming when there is a jellyfish invasion. Be sure to follow the rules and protect yourself those nasty stings. Smoking indoors is prohibited, so be sure to keep that in mind. The fine for smoking in public places can be up to €500, so it is definitely not worthy it to be engaged in such activities. If you are interested in purchasing antiquities from this part of Greece, keep in mind that there are strict custom regulations to be taken into consideration.

The Greek Islands are located in an active seismic zone – even though no serious earthquakes have occurred in the last years, there are frequent tremors (normal seismic activity). Many of the islands have confronted with widespread forest fires in the past few years – if you are visiting wooded areas, you must act in a manner that is 100% responsible (no barbecues, no lighting fires).

Did you ever hear the saying: "When in Rome, do as the Romans"? Well, if you have decided to travel to the Greek Islands, you must respect the local customs and traditions, including those that are related to tradition. Keep in mind that all travelers have to be culturally sensitive, as this is the right thing to do. The Greeks are Orthodox, so do not be surprise to see a lot of shrines on the road and people signing the cross.

Chapter 5: Transportation opportunities on the Greek Islands

Credits: Pixabay.com

The majority of the tourists travel by air from their home country, reaching Athens through different international carriers. From Athens, the most common method of transportation is the ferry. This method of

31

transportation is also used when traveling between the different Greek Islands. If you are wondering about the possibility of traveling by air, you should know that there are very few island connections. There are only several connections available, provided by small carriers, such as Sky Express (http://www.skyexpress.gr/). However, if you decide to travel by air from one island to the other, you should know that these small airliners cover the Cyclades, the Aegean Islands, Dodecanese and Crete. Keep in mind that, due to the fact you are traveling in a small plane, there is a luggage limitation (max. 12 kg).

One of the most important companies that provides ferry transportation on the Greek Islands is Bluestar (http://www.bluestarferries.com/). The ferries leave Athens and they reach the most important Greek Islands. You can also travel with the ferries provided by Hellenic Seaways (http://www.hellenicseaways.gr/). This company has both catamarans and hydrofoils to offer as methods of transportation, reaching the Cyclades, Sporades Islands and the Saronic Gulf. If you are interested in fast catamaran travels, you should consider traveling with Sea Jets (http://www.seajets.gr/). The ferries from Sea Jets leave Athens (Piraeus or Rafina ports) and they reach the Cyclades, Crete or Santorini. They can also be used for travels between the different Greek Islands. Last, but not least, there is Nel Lines (http://www.nel.gr/). This company has ferries with complex schedules, reaching the Cyclades (eastern and central islands) and the islands located in the north-east part of the Aegean Sea.

Thanks to the development of the Internet, it is possible to check out the schedules of the ferries in advance and book your tickets online. There are several websites that you can visit for such purposes, including: http://www.ferries.gr/; http://www.danae.gr/; http://www.ferriesingreece.com/. Keep in mind that there are some ferries that have the tickets classified according to class, with economy tickets being available to those interested. Cabin accommodation is possible for the slower or the overnight ferries. If you decide to travel with the ferries from Bluestar or Nel, remember that there are pre-assigned economy seats available (the additional cost is minimal, so it is totally worth it). The majority of the catamarans have designated seating, providing you with fast travel.

If you know yourself to suffer from sea sickness, it is for the best to choose a larger or traditional ferry for your trip to the Greek Islands. These ferries are large in size and they are not affected by the bad weather. Plus, they are not canceled when there are strong winds on the sea. By choosing a large ferry, despite the increased strength of the wind, you will have a smooth journey and reach the desired Greek Islands safely.

Depending on how acquainted you are with sailing, it is also possible to reach the Greek Islands by chartering your own sailing boat or yacht. Motorboats are also available upon demand. Keep in mind that you can also rent a boat together with a charter crew and travel between the different Greek Islands. In deciding upon such endeavors, you will also have to take your budget into consideration.

It is also possible to travel with smaller water taxis, as these are widely available, especially when it comes to going from one island to the other. The water taxis are especially recommended to those who are interested in reaching the Greek islands that are very small or those that are located in remote areas. The prices are quite reasonable and you will surely find the journey to be more pleasant than you imagined it in the first place. The water taxis remain a convenient method of exploring the Greek Islands, especially when it comes to the remote beaches.

As you have reached the desired destination, there are several methods of transportation available on the island. The taxis on the island have reasonable prices as well and most of them are equipped with navigation systems, so you can reach any address without stress. Keep in mind that the rates double at night and that there are many taxis without meters – if you do not want to end up paying a small fortune for your transportation, it is for the best to establish the price of the journey before getting in.

The bus service is also available on the majority of the Greek Islands. The main bus stations are often located in the vicinity of the ports and, at the peak season, you can find a detailed map with all the routes, bus stops and time schedules in the station. The driver of the bus is also a fountain of information, especially if you are looking to reach certain points of interest on the island. The price of the ticket varies according to the final destination and the tickets can either be purchased at kiosks or onboard, directly from the driver. Even though the bus service is sometimes slow, it is can be a great alternative to other methods of transportation. Instead of getting annoyed in traffic or trying desperately to find a parking spot, you can take the bus and reach the beach without any additional stress.

Apart from the taxis and the buses, you can always rent scooters, mopeds or motorcycles. There are numerous rental services available and they also provide insurance for the vehicle in question. The rental services can also be useful if you are interested in covering the island by bike or car. Make sure that you read the rental agreement in detail, so that you know the terms and conditions and what happens in case of an accident. Having travel insurance is quite useful in such situations, as it can cover the expenses related to accidents. Also, keep in mind that there are many small islands where no method of transportation is available. These are easily covered on foot and the exercise can do you a lot of good.

Chapter 6: The best hotels and restaurants on the Greek Islands

Credits: Pixabay.com

When it comes to finding accommodation on any of the Greek Islands, there are hundreds of possibilities to be taken into consideration. Given the diversity of tourists who come to visit the Greek Islands, it is not surprising to discover that the same island can offer high-end luxury hotels and affordable hostels at the same time.

37

Let's find out more information on the best hotels that welcome guests on the Greek Islands.

These are the best hotels on the different Greek Islands:

- Mediterraneo (Kastelorizo Island)
    - Charming hotel, located in an old, renovated waterfront mansion
    - Colorful décor
    - Bedrooms overlook the harbor
    - Sunbathing terrace available to all guests
    - Bathing ladder provides access directly to the sea
    - Lavish breakfast serves every morning
    - Address: Kastelorizo, Dodekanes, 85111
    - Tel.: +302246049007
    - Website: http://www.mediterraneo-megisti.com/

- Villa Faros (Lesvos)
    - Located on a private peninsula
    - Excellent yoga and spa facilities
    - Access to three private beaches
    - Seawater infinity pool and heated indoor wave pool
    - Fresh fruits and vegetables from the garden

- o Speedboat and helipad available to all guests
  - o Address: Sigris Lesvos
  - o Website: http://www.unique-resorts.com/

- Argentikon Luxury Suites (Chios)
  - o 8 luxury suites decorated in the medieval Italian style
  - o Gardens with citrus trees and rose bushes
  - o Outdoor pool available to all guests
  - o Excellent restaurant with wines available from the winery on the premises
  - o Fitness center, sauna and whirlpool
  - o Rooms equipped with air conditioning and fireplaces
  - o Private car transfers from the airport
  - o Address: Kampos, 82100
  - o Tel.: +302271033111
  - o Website: http://argentikon.gr/

- The Bay Estate (Corfu)
  - o 10-people capacity for each villa
  - o Housekeeper available for the guests
  - o Private chef and host
  - o Infinity pool and access to secluded beach

- o Best blend between high-end hotel services and intimacy
- o Address: Kerasia, Corfu
- o Website: http://www.cvvillas.com/

- Katikies (Santorini)
  - o 29 rooms available
  - o Amazing infinity pool
  - o Accommodation offered in cottages carved out of volcanic rock
  - o Exquisite gourmet restaurant
  - o Vintage wines tastings organized for guests
  - o The staff is both friendly and efficient
  - o Address: Oia, Santorini
  - o Tel.: +302286071
  - o Website: http://www.villakatikies-santorini.com/

- Adrina Beach Resort & Spa (Sporades Islands)
  - o Amazing resort hotel located on the Skopelos Island
  - o Family-owned and run hotel
  - o Private beach area available to hotel guests
  - o Seawater swimming pool

- o Taverna-style restaurant, with traditional Greek cuisine
- o Rooms with garden or sea view
- o Address: Skopelos, 37003
- o Tel.: +302424023373
- o Website: http://www.adrinaresort.com/

- Agalia Luxury Suites (Ios)
  - o Beautiful location, overlooking the beach
  - o Exclusive boutique hotel
  - o The attractions of the island are within a short distance
  - o Stylish restaurant – Greek and fusion cuisine
  - o Bespoke concierge services – port transfers, private rentals of the beach and boat trips
  - o Address: Tzamaria, 84001
  - o Tel.: +306970114922
  - o Website: http://www.agaliahotel.com/

- Al Mare Villas (Rhodes)
  - o Located on Kiotari Beach
  - o Fully-equipped apartments with access to private beach
  - o Each apartment has its own terrace overlooking the beach

- o Outdoor pool available to all guests
- o Horse riding trips and water sports organized for hotel guests
- o Address: Kiotari Beach 1, 85109
- o Tel.: +302244047130
- o Website: http://www.almarevillas.com/

- Almyra Guest Houses (Mykonos)
  - o Luxury accommodation in a peaceful location
  - o All the suites have a private veranda, providing a spectacular view over the Aegean Sea
  - o Luxury maisonette available to those interested
  - o Access to private beach
  - o Free shuttle service upon request
  - o Address: Paraga, 84600
  - o Tel.: +306936104552
  - o Website: http://www.almyraguesthouses.com/

- AVLI Lounge Apartments (Crete)
  - o Located in a renovated building, dating from the 16th Century
  - o Luxury boutique hotel

- o Variety of water sports available for hotel guests
- o The apartments retain many of their original features
- o All necessary amenities available
- o Address: Xanthoudidou 22, Rethimno, 74100
- o Tel.: +302831058250
- o Website: http://www.avli.gr/.

When it comes to food, the Greek cuisine is well-known for its delicious taste and the dishes that have authentic flavors. Below, you will find information on the best restaurants that are located on the different Greek Islands. Do not hesitate to try them out!

These are the best restaurants on the Greek Islands:

- Old Fortress Restaurant (Corfu)
  - o Magnificent scenery – grand Venetian fortress
  - o Traditional Greek cuisine, including Corfiot cuisine
  - o Amazing view over the Garitsa Bay and the Ionian Sea
  - o Exquisite dining experience
  - o Best place for local delicacies
  - o Address: Corfu, Ionian Islands, 49083

43

- o Tel.: +302661042279
- o Website:
  http://www.corfuoldfortress.com/

- Alekos (Crete)
  - o Secluded tavern, located in a traditional village
  - o Recommended choices – sautéed snails with garlic and rosemary, goat dishes
  - o For certain dishes, pre-ordering is necessary
  - o House wine available upon request
  - o Address: Vori, Crete
  - o Tel.: +302892091094
  - o Website:
    http://www.tavernalekos.blogspot.com/

- Venus Restaurant Bar (Ios)
  - o Located on the Manganari beach
  - o Family-run restaurant
  - o Delicious cuisine, prepared from fresh, locally-grown ingredients
  - o Excellent wine selection
  - o Address: Manganari Beach, Ios
  - o Website: http://www.venus-hotel.gr/

- Mavrikos (Rhodes)

- o Located in the main square of Lindos
- o Family-run restaurant
- o The dishes are defined by simplicity, with amazing flavors
- o Popular among tourists and locals as well
- o Tradition of culinary excellence
- o Address: Lindos, 85107
- o Tel.: +302244031232

- Mesogeios Restaurant (Thassos)
  - o Located in Limenas, the capital of Thassos
  - o Excellent location, in the port area, near the sea
  - o Best quality for the dishes prepared in this restaurant
  - o Address: Limenas, 64004
  - o Tel.: +302593023319
  - o Website: http://www.mesogeios-thassos.com/

- Axiotissa (Naxos)
  - o Best place for organic cuisine
  - o All dishes are prepared from locally-grown ingredients
  - o Recommended choices – cheese platter, sautéed mushrooms, aubergine with almonds and pine nuts

- o Fresh seafood used traditional dishes
- o Excellent wine and beer selection
- o Address: 18 km of the Naxos town center
- o Tel.: +302285075107

- Kikis Tavern (Mykonos)
    - o Located near the Agios Sostis beach
    - o Locally-run Greek tavern
    - o Fresh food, prepared on charcoal barbeques
    - o Recommended choices – grilled local fish, traditional meat dishes
    - o Amazing view, overlooking the ocean
    - o Address: Agios Sostis Beach, Mykonos

- Olive Land (Skiathos)
    - o Mouth-watering dishes prepared from locally-grown ingredients
    - o Breathtaking views from above
    - o Recommended choice – olive dip with fresh baked bread, risotto
    - o Excellent wine selection
    - o Delicious desserts to be tasted and enjoyed
    - o Address: Katsarou, 37002
    - o Tel.: +302427023149

- Akrotiri Tavern (Zakynthos)
    - Delicious, traditional Greek dishes
    - Starter plate offered with an amazing variety of choices
    - Recommended choices as main course – souvlaki, veal or pork chops, grilled meat
    - Excellent selection of red and white wines
    - Address: Akrotiri, Zakynthos
    - Tel.: +302695045712

- Selene (Santorini)
    - Located in the beautiful village of Pyrgos
    - Recommended choices – sea urchin, artichoke salad, dishes with local, wild capers
    - Excellent fish stew to be savored
    - Amazing desserts – yoghurt or ice cream with honey
    - Address: Pyrgos, Santorini
    - Tel.: +302286022249
    - Website: http://www.selene.gr/.

Chapter 7: The cultural highlights of the Greek Islands

Credits: Pixabay.com

The cultural calendar is filled to the maximum on the Greek Islands, especially during the summer. No matter which of the Greek Islands you decide to visit, you will have the pleasant surprise to discover that there are numerous cultural events to occupy your time with. Many of these events are concentrated on music and

49

drama, satisfying the tastes and personal preferences of even the most pretentious visitor.

The island of Santorini has many splendid cultural events that are worth checking out. Every August, you take part in the Megaro Gyzi Festival (http://www.megarogyzi.gr/). Organized at the Megaro Gyzi Cultural Centre in Fira, this cultural event includes a wide range of music concerts, theater performances, art exhibitions and splendid lectures. Speaking about Santorini cultural events, you can also take part in the Santorini Biennale (http://www.santorinibiennale.gr/). The next one is going to take part between September-October 2016, with "Alice in Wonderland" as the main theme. If you want to discover an event that is dedicated to art and culture, celebrating diversity at the same time, the Santorini Biennale is the right choice.

As it was already mentioned, summer is the period in which the majority of the cultural events take place on the Greek Islands. If you want a unique experience, you should consider the Naxos Festival (http://www.bazeostower.gr/). Organized every July and August, in Bazeos Tower, this event entices visitors from all over the world with amazing musical performances, theatre plays and art exhibitions. Attendees have the opportunity to enjoy lectures from reputed artists and also to take part in the art workshops, so the experience is 100% enthralling.

Between 20th and 22nd of August, on the island of Paros, the event known as "Routes in Marpissa" is organized. This is indeed a one-of-a-kind event that you do not want to miss out. As a cultural festival, this event centers on four important themes meaning music, architecture, sculpture and environment. During the period of this original festival, one can take part in action games, art workshops and concerts. The event is completed with projections and exhibitions.

Do you like film festivals? If the answer is yes, you should consider Anima Syros (http://www.animasyros.gr/). This is an International Animation Festival, organized at the end of September. Apart from the animated short films, guests have the opportunity to take part in educative workshops and also in a wide-range of events dedicated to the animation art. Many of these events are focused on the hosting city – Hermoupolis – so this should definitely be an interesting experience. Speaking about film festivals, the International Short Tourism Film Festival is also worth checking out (http://www.yperia.gr/). Organized in the middle of October, in Aigiali, on the Amorgos Island, this festival intends to encourage tourism through the usage of media. Films and documentaries are presented during this event, with awards being given to those who were previously nominated. This film festival also uses the occasion in order to highlight what different tourist areas have to offer, addressing important issues related to tourist at the same time.

The theater is an important part of the Greek culture and many of the cultural events including amazing, dramatic performances. One of the most interesting events of this sort is the Philippi Festival (http://www.philippifestival.gr/). Organized on the island of Thasos, this is a festival dedicated to classical drama, taking place between July and August. With an excellent location – the ancient theater of Philippi – this event is excellent for those with a passion for classical drama but also for those who are more interested in seeing modern plays. During this event, you also have the opportunity to take part in music concerts and see photo exhibitions that are a true display of talent and creativity.

Music enthusiasts should consider taking part in the Samos Young Artists Festival (http://www.schwartzfoundation.com/). Taking place in Samos, for one week in August, this event is quite a pleasant surprise for tourists of different ages and occupations. With a unique location – the ancient theater outside the Phythagorio resort – this event entices with amazing performances bearing the trademark signature of international artists. If you want to listen to classical piano, jazz or opera, there is no better event to check out and be a part of.

Both children and adults can enjoy the Puppet Festival that is organized each year in Hydra (http://www.hydra.com/). This is an annual festival that takes place each and every July, welcoming experienced and dedicated puppeteers from all over the world. If you want to see amazing displays of talent and art, this event is the right choice.

Speaking about annual festivals, I also recommend the Kyrvia Festival (http://www.ierapetra.net/). Organized each year in Ierapetra, this festival takes place between July and August, providing attendees with a wide range of cultural activities. The guests of the festival have the opportunity to see the most incredible singing and dancing performances, not to mention a wide range of music concerts, screenings to popular films and unique theater performances.

The Frikaria Music Festival is just as interesting to visit, attracting tourists from all over the world (http://www.frikariafestival.tk/). This event lasts for three days, being organized at the end of July or at the start of August. During the three days, you have the opportunity to listen to some of the most important Greek bands singing rock and also to amazing DJs. Organized in Agios Kirykos, it is the perfect event for a hot summer spent on the Greek Islands.

After having read about the cultural events that are organized on the different Greek Islands, you have probably understood that diversity is the key word. If you are passionate about music, theater and art in general, there are countless events that you can visit. These cultural events are going to help you create ever-lasting memories regarding the time you have spent on the Greek Islands, memories that you are going to cherish for the rest of your life. Island hopping is going to become even more interesting, as you will go from one cultural event to the other.

Chapter 8: Shopping on the Greek Islands

Credits: Pixabay.com

Shopping on any of the Greek Islands is a genuine pleasure, with each island having the most incredibly variety to offer to its visitors. The majority of the shopping is, as you will have the opportunity to see on your own, concentrated on the souvenirs that reflect the local culture and tradition. Whether you are interested in finding a keepsake for yourself or you

55

want to purchase something for the loved ones back at home, it is guaranteed that you will be pleasantly impressed with the selection offered.

Crete is one of the best places to shop, especially when it comes to the weekly markets. Opened from early morning until the afternoon, these markets provide tourists with the opportunity to taste fresh, local fruits and vegetables. Moreover, they are the best place to shop for local crafts and souvenirs. I especially recommend visiting Hania's market, as it has everything you could ever wish for. Purchase the locally-made honey and be sure to stock up on traditional Greek drinks, such as ouzo or raki. These markets are great if you are shopping for leatherwork or traditional ceramic souvenirs. On Saturday, there are special markets organized – from there, you can purchase local fruits (caplosca), Greek cheese (feta, kefalotiri) and tea (dictamus tea).

The Heraklion District of Crete is especially popular among tourists, given the impressive variety of products that is offered here. Many tourists visit this district in order to discover the latest designer label clothing, not to mention the exquisite jewelry items and the fine antiques. The shops here also provide high-quality leather goods at the most amazing prices. The Chania District is perfect when it comes to shopping for jewelry, leather products and souvenirs of all sorts. Whether you want to purchase traditional Greek fabrics, crafted pottery or artwork, it is guaranteed that you will be pleased with the choices presented.

If you find yourself in Santorini, keep in mind that this island is famous for its jewelry. While there are many shops selling jewelry, one of the most popular ones is Nakis. In Fira, while walking on the small, cobbled streets, you will discover many shops – these sell a wide range of products, including high-end jewelry and cheap souvenirs. On the other hand, if you go to Oia, you will find this part of Santorini to be ideal for purchasing contemporary art pieces. Hand-crafted original jewelry can also be purchased from the island of Rhodes or Sifnos – just make sure you time your time and browse all of the existent shops.

While Rhodes is extremely crowded when it comes to shopping, you do have the opportunity to shop for unique souvenirs at the best possible prices. Among the recommended choices, there are the ouzo drinks housed in the quirkiest bottles, the beaded jewelry and the Greek olive soap. The shopping experience on the Rhodes Island has variety written all over it. Shoppers can find top brand clothing at attractive prices but also more affordable items of clothing housed in local boutiques. The leatherwork, including belts, shoes and handbags, is abundant in Rhodes and it comes to complete the overall shopping experience. The good news is that you can also find top-quality, local craftwork at cheap prices. You can purchase unique wood carvings or embroidered fabrics for your friends and family, offering these gifts as traditional Greek souvenirs.

Speaking about souvenirs, if you visit the island of Sifnos, be sure to check out the pottery shops. Sifnos has an ancient tradition when it comes to pottery and there are many local artisans selling such products at souvenirs to those interested. Given the fact that this island is not so touristy, you can also take advantage of the low prices.

On many of the Greek Islands, you will find icon paintings of saints offered as souvenirs. You need to remember that these are part of the Orthodox Christian faith, with a tradition that is quite powerful. If you want to purchase such souvenirs, you should know that you have two choices available. You either purchase the souvenirs that are mass-produced (which are cheaper) or you decide to go with the items made by individual craftsmen (given the intense work associated with making such products, these items tend to be more expensive). On the island of Patmos, as well as on Rhodes, you can find an excellent selection of icons and purchase them as souvenirs.

When shopping for leather, there are many islands that you can visit, as this is one of the Greek specialties. I especially recommend visiting Symi Island, as this is not that crowded and the prices for leather products are excellent. Moreover, you will surely be pleasantly impressed with the quality of the belts and purses that are made on this island. Like in many other situations, taking your time to talk to the owner and being friendly can guarantee a better price for the items purchased.

If you are interested in offering a unique souvenir, perhaps you might be interested in natural sponges. These are taken out of the sea and dried through specific techniques, being offered for sale as unique souvenirs. Some of the best natural sponges are to be found on the island of Karpathos and Symi; you can pair them with a bar of olive oil soap purchased from Crete and offer to a person you appreciate or love. The spices that are found on Symi island also make up for the ideal gift – you will certainly not resist the temptation of purchasing some for yourself, adding unique flavors to your Greek salad, fish dishes and grilled meat (try the ones recommended for grilled lamb, as they truly bring out the flavor of the meat).

Mykonos is the ideal Greek island to visit in case you want to shop for stylish clothing. The good news is that the stores have prolonged opening hours, so you do not cut into your beach time in order to go shopping. The available choices are extremely varied, ranging from souvenir T-shirts to items of clothing belonging to international designer brands. On the plus side, if you are visiting Mykonos in August, you can take delight in the lovely summer sales. The souvenir stores are also great to be visited, providing prospective customers with varied choices, including handmade jewelry, traditional prints and Greek beverages, such as ouzo.

Chapter 9: The portrait of the Greek Islands

Credits: Pixabay.com

Someone once said that Greece is the most magical place on Earth. Given the fact that there are over 200 Greek Islands that are inhabited and available for visits, it is safe to assume that each of these islands is a small paradise on its own. Tourists from all over the world come here to enjoy the warm climate, bathing in the sun and dipping into the crystal-clear sea. The

61

Greek Islands entice with the unique landscape, with kilometers of sandy beaches, sheltered bays and caves, not to mention the rocky landscape and the volcanic soil.

The beaches on the Greek Islands are perfect for sunbathing and swimming there is a genuine pleasure, as the waters are completely safe. The appeal of these beaches increases threefold when it comes to the wide range of water sports that are available to each and every tourist. Among the most popular choices, one can find scuba diving, windsurfing, sailing, water skiing and snorkeling. First-timers are welcomed to try these water sports, with experienced instructors introducing them to the basics.

But coming to the Greek Islands is not just about bathing in the sun and engaging in water sports. You are going to the European cradle of culture, as many of the Greek Islands have a genuinely rich heritage. Some of the oldest civilizations of Europe have made Greece their home and their traces are still visible today. There are numerous archaeological sites that can be visited, providing an insight into the world of ancient civilizations such as the Minoans or the Cycladic civilization. The architectural heritage is reason enough to visit the Greek Islands but surely not the only one.

The Greek Islands have a unique flavor, with their fascinating local traditions, friendly people and age-old customs. A vacation spent on any of the Greek Islands will bring you the necessary relaxation. Walking on the cobbled streets, taking a look at the whitewashed houses with their blue roofs and windows, you will feel like you have stepped back in time. The laid back style of living is to be appreciated and, as a tourist, you cannot help but try it out as well. After a few days spent on any of the Greek Islands, you will feel both relaxed and energized.

The food is an inherent part of the Greek culture. Everyone knows that the Greek cuisine is appreciated all over the world, as it has an authentic flavor and taste. During your stay on the island, you will have the opportunity to taste authentic dishes at their finest. Many of the Greek taverns prepare dishes from locally-grown ingredients, so you will surely fall in love with the fresh taste. Just think about the delicious olive oil, the fresh homemade bread and the amazing seafood. Mouthwatering dishes are going to complete your traveling experience, creating memories that you are going to hold dear in your heart. Food is sensual in Greece, with many dishes having aphrodisiac properties. Apart from that, all the meals are paired with an excellent selection of alcoholic beverages, whether we are talking about wine, ouzo or raki.

The Greeks are extremely friendly people and they are more than happy in talking to tourists. When shopping, you will discover that you can obtain discounts on different items just by being attentive and polite. They are just as friendly in the restaurants or bars, always being interested in a lively conversation. The Greek traditional nights that are organized in different restaurants are totally worth it, as you will have the time of your life. Yes, it is true that you will smash a plate or two but you will definitely have a lot of fun.

Some of the Greek Islands, such as Ios, are known for the amazing nightlife. If you are interested in dancing and having fun, do not hesitate to check out the clubs and the open beach bars that are found there. You can find young people who have come here from different parts of the world, being interested in the same things as yourself. Many of them are backpackers, so they can introduce you to this experience as well.

Other Greek Islands are not so touristy but they offer a peaceful and relaxing atmosphere. Some of these islands have private beaches, with solitary villas providing the possibility for a romantic stay. Depending on your budget, you can even decide to rent your own island and have the time of your life. On the other hand, if you are prefer to be with a lot of people, islands such as Corfu, Crete or Rhodes are known for being a tourist magnet.

On the Greek Islands, life seems to be going at a slower pace. No one is in a hurry to get to work and the lunch time is reserved for relaxation. If you want a place to relax and unwind, this is the vacation that you need to take. Whether you want to bathe in the sun, go on hiking trips or try out different water sports, it is guaranteed that this holiday is going to rejuvenate you.

The Greek Islands are small slices of paradise. Nature seems to have reached perfection in this part of the world, with pristine beaches and secluded bays welcoming those who are interested in relaxing and nothing more. More or less difficult hiking trails invite those with a passion for the outdoors to discover the Greek Islands panorama from up above. Taking photographs is a pleasure, as there are so many beautiful things to capture on camera.

After a few days spent on any of the Greek Islands, you will feel like you have always been there. The more time you will spend on the island, the more of the local customs and relaxed air you will borrow. You will appreciate the Greek for the laid-back way of life, promising to yourself to return the next summer for a new encounter with this amazing destination.

PS: Please leave your review

If you reached this last page, probably this travel guide has given you some ideas about your stay in Barcelona!!

Would you be kind enough to leave a review for this book on Amazon? It will help other travelers to find their way through this beautiful country!

Many thanks and enjoy your trip!

monetary loss due to the information herein, either directly or indirectly.

Respective authors own all copyrights not held by the publisher.

The information herein is offered for informational purposes solely, and is universal as so. The presentation of the information is without contract or any type of guarantee assurance.

The trademarks that are used are without any consent, and the publication of the trademark is without permission or backing by the trademark owner. All trademarks and brands within this book are for clarifying purposes only and are the owned by the owners themselves, not affiliated with this document.

Made in the USA
Las Vegas, NV
13 April 2021